NEW POETRY ANTHOLOGY I

NEW POETRY ANTHOLOGY I

edited by Michael Anania

THE **SWALLOW PRESS** INC.

CHICAGO

PUBLISHED BY
THE SWALLOW PRESS INCORPORATED
1139 SOUTH WABASH AVENUE
CHICAGO, ILLINOIS 60605

ACKNOWLEDGMENTS

The publisher wishes to thank the magazines
which have given permission to reprint the
following poems:

Barbara Harr's "Rapid Transit," from *Gallery
Series/two*. Copyright © 1968 by *Gallery
Series*.

Richard Lourie's "What Herodotus Told Me
About the Persian Empire," from *Chicago
Review*, Vol. 20 no. 1. Copyright © 1968 by
Chicago Review.

James McMichael's "1/15," from *West Coast
Review*, Fall 1968; "5/20," from *The Colorado
State Review*, Fall 1968; "8/26," from *Poetry:
An Introductory Anthology*, edited by Hazard
Adams (Little, Brown and Company);
"10/12," *The North American Review*, No-
vember-December 1968; "10/17," *The Denver
Quarterly*, Spring 1966; "12/25," *The South-
ern Review*, Spring 1967.

Dennis Schmitz' "(3) Poems Done in the
Ancient Manner Beginning with the Spurious
Fragment 'After the Battle'," from *Chicago
Review*, Vol. 20 no. 1. Copyright © 1968 by
Chicago Review.

LIBRARY OF CONGRESS CATALOG NO. 69-20470

TABLE OF CONTENTS

PREFACE / vii

Dennis Schmitz / 1
    our ancestors watch / 3
    On a Reef That Ship / 4
    Complaint & Refrain / 5
    Saddle the Itineries Read / 6
    A Love Poem. Mitchell, South, Dakota / 7
    crated / 8
    (3) Poems Written in the Ancient Manner Beginning
        With the Spurious Fragment "After the Battle" / 9

William Moebius / 13
    Elegy 7 / 15
    Elegy 9 / 19
    Ode 10 / 22

Peter Michelson / 25
    from Pacific Plainsong
        Preface to the Works of H. H. Bancroft / 27
        "Though coming to them under color of peace" / 30
        On the Beach at Lapush / 32
        Leschi, scene treatment for a many humored musicale / 34
        "Seattle is described as a dignified and venerable personage" / 39

James McMichael / 45
    from What To Do When the Rivers Freeze
        1/15 / 47
        1/19 / 48
        5/20: Intimations of Heart-Seizure / 49
        8/26 / 51
        9/22: A Passion / 52
        10/12 / 53
        10/17: Breughel's "Seven Sins" / 54

12/8: Bobby / 55
12/25: In a Graveyard: Bodie, California / 56

Richard Lourie / 57
What Herodotus Told Me About the Persian Empire / 59
radio / 62
dreaming of Queens / 63
sex in America / 64
cancion / 65
On Visitation Day / 66
bad day together / 67

Barbara Harr / 69
Rapid Transit / 71
Returning Late Past the Subway Shops / 72
Clark Street / 73
Power / 74
The American Children / 75
Juana Guitarist / 76
The Dresses / 77
Juana: The Burnt Foot / 79

Charles Doria / 81
from The Game of Europe
Introduction / 83
The Vienna Chapters I-IIII / 88

Michael Anania / 95
from Stops Along the Western Bank of the Missouri
A Journal / 97
The Fall / 100
Songs from an Institution (1 and 3) / 103
Memorial Day / 105
A Second-Hand Elegy / 106

AFTERWORD / 107

PREFACE

This volume marks the beginning of an annual series of Swallow NEW POETRY ANTHOLOGIES. The program's purpose is to introduce new poets in a less congested format than is otherwise available, giving them enough space to make their ways with the reader. In order to narrow the field, *new* poets are simply defined as poets who have not, at the time of submission, been published in book form. No other stipulations concerning age or prior success with "little magazines" have been made, and though the contributors were urged to send unpublished work, previous magazine publication did not exclude poems essential to a representative or coherent selection of the poets' work.

Of course, *new* is also used in another sense, to place upon the poet again Ezra Pound's burden—*Make It New*. Every poetic vogue is worthy of our distrust, every critical entrenchment worthy of slander, but making it new is the only possible alchemy for change.

There is no pretense here toward the comprehensive, no ambition in a single volume to document the goings on in every poetic corner in the country. It is hoped that over the years an accumulation of these anthologies will reflect the changes now inevitable in our poetry and present new opportunities to the men and women who have set themselves the task of change.

M. A.

Dennis Schmitz

DENNIS SCHMITZ was born in Dubuque, Iowa in 1937 and attended Loras College and The University of Chicago. He lives in Sacramento and teaches English at Sacramento State College. Mr. Schmitz' poems have appeared in most of the magazines seriously publishing new poetry, and have been anthologized in *Heartland: Poets of the Midwest* and *The Young American Poets*. The manuscript of his first book, *The Rescue*, has won the Big Table Younger Poets Prize and will be published by Follett in 1969.

our ancestors watch

face mirrors appear
        everywhere guide-books
tell the ways through
a man's heart
was entered elsewhere his father
        proves these pieces
this luggage he leaves the heart
        is a station along the way we see
our mother's organs these
adornments
these walks when after the rain
        returns some child
falls
we note someone else's face on
the other penis
        in the mirror requires
        this much
love is left

ON A REEF THAT SHIP

abandoned
surmised as a fear
of water I sing
like a native of the dead
the scrap ship rides
out its own
anticipation the new land

I stand on connecting
the waves moving
sand in and out, edged

holes arrive before the waters
pick up

the passengers
die in the exits doors
were the first
holes the finger makes tears

someone else's clothes ahead of him
the water which touches
what we knew as children
but never speak about

the terror! of pushing
from the body through a tight tear
the water as much as you like
tear
at the body all of us pause
hold hands
to your own opening apply

a deep breath against the water

COMPLAINT & REFRAIN

       keys
know each other release
   some kiss keep
those who fell
away those who open
       exits from the wall-
paper we take counsels too
late
   the
       volatile body is
    emptied to the floor as you open
your shirt the key

enters
death steps in & closes you
   are still
benefiting you
later forget tear love

      between us

SADDLE THE ITINERIES READ

saddle the itineries read
up and down
like calendars some Chinese
    or CLOSED FOR IMPROVE-
MENTS the roads are all
weather cloudy passing into
    rain since you have come

this far you sit to trace
    secondaries in your wrist
sighing
in your shoes austerity recognizes
the road turning
        from known paths you see
    settlements of Christians
are lost
no longer than you were before
    the wilderness which crosses
again before you
        the day drops

a tangle the hours
track you down sniff
your familiars pick up your heart
        in a bundle of veins work

at the knots

A LOVE POEM. MITCHELL,
SOUTH DAKOTA

    my shadow
revisits the memory tries
    to carry
what you have left leave again
my dear this colony

where men fight the open
    fields enter the badlands
my shadow thrown about you
    the rocks
desire some trees

stir you leave my shadow
slips to the ground

crated.

past one
body we go from all
the rented rooms
we have ever left at first
giving back all we ever
gained our own blood who waits
with a cup what
grave outside gropes
toward you rooting
earwigs ants scissors —
beetles lapping
the thin drool of the penis
through the garden the corners
timed you toss every night
back in the hallway evict
your privates say

you are not at home to anyone

(3) POEMS DONE IN THE ANCIENT MANNER BEGINNING WITH THE SPURIOUS FRAGMENT "AFTER THE BATTLE"

we had arrived
   at the delta the dank

bodies bobbed the slow screw
     at the navel the finger
of one corpse played
in the grooves the woods

      were strained
through the green scum a face
a leaf sank

  anchored stopped
the tide-exhausted fields the dead
    caught on twigs sand
stopping their ears they sang

  in one another's arms we
separate the bodies pick the hair
from our faces
    placenta & the nests

alike we float
      fluid in our noses the last
breath is steeped
   delta the five passages
the three returns blotted before

     us the eternal
shrinking the water bugs
in our underwear
  we reach down to be sure

II

on land the ravens float
up in the shadows of the wastes shovels
were not enough the tissues

    you will need
  holidays to recover
the urine a small stone jar cooled
    he said being a veteran
green yet

  r:pe heart
of eucalyptus we brought sacks
for our own needs the beasts behaved
    violently in the fields
there were tracks in
the ravines droppings
  moist yellow cones soldier
    ants bearing leaves against
the wind their own white

    dots foulings signs it was
the spring winds
    turned

III

my dear send
  he wrote five difficult signs
here the bread
  one breaks open with weevils another
wonder the fowl are gray & white

    markings on their privates
indicate upriver
  grain in the marsh-

fly's bite one soldier
    who thought he fought
for right one will fuck
    other animals will not

allow such behavior the sage
   said out of the line
out of the straight can one work
the core

   indicates the size
fruit burns one
   used to simple water our armor
must now be soaked
in spare plasma which a man bears

then to our master
   who far away does not hear
nor send funds

William Moebius

WILLIAM MOEBIUS was born in Milwaukee in 1941 and attended Lawrence University, Columbia, and SUNY at Buffalo. He lives in Amherst and teaches comparative literature at the University of Massachusetts. One of his Odes was published in *The Niagara Frontier Review*, and his verse translation of *Oedipus at Colunus* will be included in an anthology of Greek drama scheduled to appear next year. His first book of poetry, *Elegies and Odes*, will be published in 1969 by The Swallow Press.

ELEGY 7

I

Hours lie ahead for the possession
of weary-eyed past. Time taps slowly
more than the ambulance, that sirens
each, taps each stoplight, crosswalk,
mewling a casualty to a final reststop,
pouring its cup of pule into the air
of daylight or nighttime. Wandering
with spectacles lost, crossing apparitions
and transportations at late-evening,
holding a spatula to wave with, kleenex
to hold my tongue, airplane glue dripping
from out of my sleek aluminum nostrils,
I seek inhabitation at Helen's Starry;
my head falls, like a deputized master
who does not want to make the dog yelp,
nor put more welts on the mistress' flesh.

From wonder-dropping Clio's quarters,
in the flames about one staggering light-year
away from holy earth, I come, to cash in
on a run-in with war and instability.

Holy house-father, (masquerade suggestion!)
I don't know what to ask, what question:
I am in spatial decline, and animal increase,
I damn well don't know how to break the lease.

Watch out! Helen is in the lane.
In danger I will cross the ice
to find out her living name, and not
her false signature, her resignation.

II

There are many hours left;
the fighting has stopped.
I do not hear the men cursing —
the trenches quiet now,
a small-town neighborhood.
I would like to give these sentences
the power to reach the ears
behind those sideburns,
only quietly I must approach them,
giving them no sermons in rag-time.

We come to this run-in with war
on a beach where guerrillas are testing
new firearms and penny gum,
purchases from a new wrench
cracking a welded nation;
isolated bodies in stale marshes
meshed in the mud that proves them
dead, mud no shot of lime
or whiskey clears, nor the kiss of sun
one feels in shortsleeves on a tractor
during summer's mid-day, nor children
shrieking on their way to class again.

III

She should not have met division,
devising of impotent and inferior deities,
that draws men in, unless she has each month
to weep into, the bower of each month,
the carriage and pitcher of each month:
I know her in her darker colors.
Men wait ages for a sort of groomed
appearance, talcum in their hair:
what happens when it's the dust
of two millenia? Must they freshen up
with some great fight? I am amazed
to see the results of that broken marriage

between Helen and excellent Menelaus,
as I look into the excellent eyes of Paris:
answers come not out of shoeboxes,
except by chance, but out of experience . . .
They that lie there, greeting the astonished Germans
with a diptheric smile, two students
with no desire to fight for Germany,
being Dutchmen, have no ideas better
than this one, plotted by their mother
and unmarried sisters. Plot to get ill
before ill, or do not plot until the illness
sets in. No man is immaculate and safe
until he is beyond the flamethrower
down in the optic and septic of Hades.

Helen in Argos again, back from abroad,
is suffering the grand award of regret,
an impossible husband afraid of Elysium,
but most of all nervousness, a tension
like the wood of a piano left out in the rain.
She is coming apart with the burials
of kids who went over to clamp down
on her wildness for friendly caress
of the stranger, for foreign haughtiness,
for fat bouquets and clever manifests,
the legacies of goddess knocker-brains,
boobs-trap, butt-butter, quiet wolverine.
Who holds out hands to that goddess?
Morons wearing quaint pointed hats,
pinecones tucked in their skirts,
running up Tmolus the Diorissimo-scented,
mixing oxygen and blood on the hot collar
of Asia, with its head in the sand.

To quiet that tired feeling in Argos,
Helen sends a posse of turtles angling
for Troy, to lay their eggs on the seashore,
and deposit her diggers of antiques,
sand-pickers, wags of the entrail circuit,
reading the past like dogs of a training

in bloodstains, as to owner of this shield,
that blackboard, or this package of signets.
The turtle-necked ramble returns
with the evidence painted on beak-prow,
in zig-zags painted on back-bone:
Helen takes it all down in embroidery,
to quiet that tired feeling in Argos.
Hail, Helen of heartbeat, intake and outthrust
of sexstream, obligation of system,
I respect you more than a harp-string,
who move the mind faster than sound,
deplorable in your sharp issue, jagged edge
of bombed-out villages, a worn-out caul.

I seek to calm the fairest of them all, in her anxiety
I know the eyestrain, the earsoreness, the headache
as the instrument palls; Helen, you have had the orientation.
How many ways to wake up are there? What formula
tells us how to see? Must we treat the sponsor nicely?
Must we be dragged by unseen powers at arm's length?

My high soul is in the well, the lover said. Anarchy
is in my brain. Follow me. That is Helen's story.

ELEGY 9

I

And I take the rap. Handle me gently.
You trouble me with burning your town.
I let the old fire out, the fireplace
crumble. No reimbursements in blood-
money. Old hairpiece swept away down
your drain. I can't stop progress,
the house specialty. Broken drainpipes,
neon temporaries, "for rent", bygones,
housepainter's wasted temerity, the clock's
prestige. Aren't you anxious with your stupid
quarrel? Hang me! Like a laxative,
when my energy is spent, you'll look at me.
Stupids! Gives you an atomic stomachache.

At daybreak he is dead. The engines
are arching from Texas. Who has resigned?
Boneweary gentlemen climb out of the hot-
rod. Lukewarm. Serene fecklessness of
broken hearts. Looney serenades. Chinese
opera, melanima, Canadian jazz.

They carried him back from the warzone,
the buddy laid out in his blood.
Bring sterling. Proliferate the zany
sunshine. Anyone can be white and strop
the razor. Zap, fap, only a few paces
behind the iron window the heads roll
in a fad of murder. The house specialty.
Blue hydrangeas droop in airtight sedans.
The summonses of Herod and percussionist.

II

I was Benito's master, you can tell them.
The captain was the slave, the slaves
on a frigate hot for Senegal. I spent

years in Africa organizing hunts
for game. I forced your kin, running
years behind you but not after you.
You come after me. It is poor timing,
the bullet guts you before the hearings.
You were short, but your eyes were squatter.
You were bright, but something pale.
A dim target in a prison corridor.
I wonder how you sleep. The black pole-
cat naps on the concrete ledge. I
sleep through trains and all other noises.
I hear and bear the photographic memory
of your animal cringing in its moving nest,
moving west. I see your animal drop
like a needle-feathered pine branch.
You're looking at a man, what a man
to kill. You've reloaded, your energy
is spent in the oceanic recoil. Your
tusks feel like rubber, you feint
from the window on the sixth story, begin
to test your legs. Your trunk, all you
held the gun with, fumbles the assembly
like a football, the gun floats loosely
to the grade c wood flooring. You tumble
out of the room, your flesh is huge, your
feet are enormous stumps, you catapult
the threshold, running an unusual errand,
a bushwhacking manhunt to escape from.
Put wounds in the preying congregation,
have the icecold passion of the lion.
A toothache, gums bleeding, when
the jawbreaking job is done. Service
the civilisation, make cessation progress.
Watch the lips flower in the jaws
of children, watch the long-sided cheeks
of old-timers emaciate. Do your thing,
while the earth is acting chaperone.

III

These are the steps and swivels I must make.
I am not bred to push the broom or open
ash-can lids to look for food. Eating
meat and vegetables, I live. Stop supplies,
I die. Baited, I hang on and fight. Caught
a man-size catch, too heavy to pull in.
Now I wriggle in this baitbox. The mantis,
or the worm? Is the temperature right?
Will there be stuff to chew? My teeth
would need wire braces; my gums are poor
without the expensive sabertooth.

Eyetooth monitors incoming traffic.
Caretaker government guards the chute
of food. Mild-tasting ointments soothe.
Trucks bring farm-fresh straight to us.
Aerated wastes are siphoned off.
Movable possessions cross the landscape
in a van; a helicopter gains the landing pad.

IV

Old revolver through with sniping, cruise me
to the countryside, a new terrain:
I want the impact of the gun flash
and the mobile loudspeakers, the pomp
of the paddy wagon, and police brutality —
I am the king in those conditions.
Impartial ears harken to our progress
on the radio — the announcer interrupts
his show — I take the microphone —
speak to each domestic privacy —
remind them of our kingdom's eagerness
to keep up with what's new, not be second-class —
I broadcast the curse, and it is carried
nationwide. Now, presidential bird,
my omen, take me to the royal site.

Put me in that revolving chair,
free me from the words I cannot use;
let my eyes close,
and turn me round and round.

I will get dizzy and protest
the giddy framework of the stool
I'm riding on
but turn me round and round.

Put your hand (you love me!)
on my neck, the other on my thigh,
and walk beside,
and turn me round and round.

I see no alternative, the gate
of my remembrance is ajar,
I open it,
you turn me round and round.

In that rotunda many people
stand around and smile
I've never met —
you turn me round and round.

I sense the mystery
beyond the microphone
these noises crowd —
you turn me round and round.

On us that they remembered
to turn back to, as we pitch forward
into darkness —
you turn me round and round —

they look ineffably, like princes,
men and women of a miracle
withheld so long —
you turn me round and round.

This is a sign of their protection,
our awe in their reflection,
our short transport,
you turn me round and round,

our amazement and the firmness
of your hand upon my neck,
upon my thigh,
you turn me round and round,

soothing me in memory
with people of one strength
and of one piece,
I see them gathered in a throng,

our ancestors, the recently deceased
no one knows about but us,
and we are here—
I see them gathered in a throng.

Peter Michelson

PETER MICHELSON was born in Chicago in
1937 and raised in Seattle. He attended the
University of Washington, Whitman College,
the University of Wyoming, and The Univer-
sity of Chicago. He lives in South Bend and
teaches English at Notre Dame. His essays and
poems have appeared in *Choice*, *Tri-Quarterly*,
North American Review, and *The New Republic*.
He was editor of *Chicago Review* from 1963 to
1965. Mr. Michelson's first book, *Pornography,
an essay in genre*, will be published next year by
Herder and Herder, and he is at work on two
poem cycles, The Eater and Pacific Plainsong.

Preface to the Works of H. H. Bancroft
Volume XXXI (History of Washington, Idaho, and Montana, 1845-1889)
pp. vi and vii

There were those determined to
serve not (as Vancouver) by
stepping on shore to luncheon and
reciting ceremonies to the
winds, nor by naming the
great River of the West for
(as Robert Gray had done)
his ship. There
were those who
served (as they determined) by
possessing there were those determined
servers determined (while securing to
themselves such homes as they might
choose) who by possessing
(of the territory) chose
to serve by taking there
were those who (by possession) chose
securely there such homes as
those (determined) who declining
luncheon and some ceremonies, chose
to serve and did (their
government) by taking territory
and (ceremonies to the winds) they
served by actual occupation.

I need not here repeat their
narrative I need not here
repeat those (bold) measures by
which these men of destiny their
destiny achieved. I
wish only to declare they
faced (those early pioneers) the
mystery, they faced the
great unknown—though (by whimsy, by
merest chance, or as we say

it fell out that) they
had found the choicest portions—
they had (of the great unknown)
found its fertile soil, its
wonderful inland sea, safe
from storms, always open to navigation,
abounding in fish, bordered
many miles wide with
the most magnificent forests on earth.

So (securing to themselves such
homes as they might choose) it
did (does) not require
a poet's vision to picture
a glowing future, albeit dim
in the reaches of time. And
to lay ever so humbly destiny's
corner-stone was worth the (humble)
toil and privation (abounding
in fish) the (safe from storms)
danger and the isolation (always
open to navigation) for
to lay destiny's corner-stone
(even) ever so humbly is worth it and
there were (weren't there)
among them those determined to serve.

Yes, and (incidentally)
this inland sea with
treasures inexhaustible of
food for the world and
fifteen hundred miles of shore covered
with pine forests to the
water's edge and
surrounding it small valleys of
the richest soils, watered
by streams from pure
snows of the Cascade
and Coast ranges, half prairie and half
forest, warm sheltered from winds enticing
the weary pilgrim from the eastern side
of the continent to rest in
their calm solitudes, so well did
God (and those who were determined to) serve

28

(though it was true that
the native wild man
still inhabited these valleys and
roamed the mountains to the number of
thirty thousand, the
incomers were sons of sires who
had met and
subdued the savage tribes of
America as they
pushed West from Plymouth Rock
to the Missouri and beyond—
therefore they had now no hesitation).

For bred to believe
that British and Indians would
melt before them they
(British and Indians melting before them)
had no hesitation and
(though there were among them
native wild men) they
(sons of savage sires) had
no hesitation and (bred to believe
in melting pots) they melted
British and Indians before
them and (determined
to serve) enticed weary pilgrims
to their calm solitudes for
there were (calm, determined) those
men of destiny facing
the great unknown there
were those bold those
determined who (securing to themselves
such as they might) chose
not (unrequired) a poet's
imagination (the British and Indians
melting) for among them were
the sons of sires determined
to serve and they (securing what
they chose) they had (picturing
a glowing future) they had therefore
(without ceremony) they had therefore now no hesitation.

The sources for this volume are those which have enabled me
to write all my volumes.

29

"Though coming to them under color of peace,
it was charged upon the chief that he intended to entrap them.
However this may have been,

the volunteers, not content with
putting so powerful an enemy out of
the way, amused themselves that evening in camp by
cutting off bits of his scalp as
trophies; and when the scalp was
entirely gone, the assistant surgeon of
the regiment cut
off his ears,
and it was said some
of his fingers . . .
Parrish probably exaggerates
when he says: They
skinned him from head to
foot, and made razor-straps of
his skin."
He (Parrish) probably
exaggerates. For it's unlikely that
the head, hands, or feet could be skinned
efficiently, the best incision (easiest) being to
cut from the neck base splaying
down the spine bypassing the rectum (arcing right
and left) across smooth buttock blubber to
the scrotum (keeping the tool flaccid and ground
ward, the indians so far as we
know being the first American sister and mother
fuckers), continue the seam down the inside of each
thigh to the ankle, encircling incisions around
ankles, privates, arms (usually not
worth their hide, excepting extraordinary
biceps) and neck, then simply peel
hide from carcass (being careful
about the ribs) and stretch to cure—though I
should note that of all skins
the human is suited more for ornamental
than productive purposes, and will not
strop a razor well, so he (Parrish) probably

exaggerates. The volunteers (perhaps) amused
themselves with bits of scalp and ears and
(it was said) some fingers, but most certainly
he (Parrish) goes too far in saying they
made razor-straps of skin. And
though the volunteers were enter-
prising men they (after all) were
men and Waiilatpu in December is
not (even today) an amusing place and
as the Walla Walla girls weren't (it may be
supposed) putting out to the enemy
the Oregon yankees (resourcefully)
amused themselves in camp, though
it would exaggerate to say they (like
Shriners) went too far and surely he (Horace
Greely) exaggerates (like Parrish) to
say (in 1858), "The enterprising territories of Oregon
and Washington have handed into congress their
little bill for scalping Indians and violating
squaws" for (as history records) truth must beware
exaggeration and most certainly they
bleed too much who say those
volunteers excessively amused
themselves in camp with
bits of scalp and ears and (it was
said) some fingers

"Thus perished the wealthy and powerful chief of the Walla Wallas."

On the Beach at Lapush

Locked in locked
in this (neither past nor
present) anachronistic village is
shrouded in its battered sea
spray air—its shoreline stacked
with stoney bleached enormous (two
feet thicker than
a man is tall) carcasses
of trees, their jagged roots upended
claw the (sullen) sky—all
all is shroud and bonewhite gleaming
along this brittle shore

A (well past bearing) squaw
rocks amid the baskets she
no longer weaves and looks beyond the mist
bound shore complaining men no longer ride
the open boats or
risk rough water out at sea.
In the village (white) Mark
Westby teaches indians (one or two) their
ancient craft of carving—offshore
Shell Oil blasts leviathon
and salmon, sounding lively
messages of profit through this pall
of spray. But I came to see
fishers at their trade, and
their past a curio,
their present obsolete

I watch the ghosts of Kwakiutl,
oil skinned and glistening, astride
the pitch and swell, they
work their dark pacific
sea and bend to haul up gleaming
nets, to bring rich flesh
of fish to air; their
calloused fingers slap the

gaff deep in the heaving
gills they snare—implaccably
they gaff that signal writhing,
                    gaff
and know an old despair.

Leschi, scene treatment for a many humored musicale

(From Telstar) camera pans
whole of continental U.S., at
Seattle zooming to
intersection of Yesler Street (original skid
road) with Elliot Bay waterfront to
(chief) Leschi, then, wearing Brando/Zapata
expression of (profound)
ennui and dedication, standing at
corner—fish trucks, tourists, and
stevedores in background, as
Mac and Muff (teeny boppers) play
(discrete) grabass, watching jellyfish
orgasm in the bay. All is
tranquil and godfearing
bustle of enterprise when
Leschi (in war paint, headress, and bear's
tooth necklace) shakes
a tambourine and bellows, "White Mother
fuckers," then (having just the night
before seen Sammy Davis Jr. as a t.v. cavalry
sergeant) adds, "Black Mother
fuckers!" All freeze agape (except Mac in slight
grimace as Muff, freezing, catches his
foreplay digit in sphincter
lock), Leschi begins war
dance, chanting Nisqually
medicine ("The times they are
achangin," punctuated at
grace notes with lyrical *White*
and/or *Black Muahfu*) and
prancing about intersection plunging
a harpoon through tires and
denting hoods and fenders with
tomahawk. All freeze until traffic cop comes
to and shouts "All right, Mac, Cut it!"
(Mac, misunderstanding, looks up
terrified, frantically doubling
efforts at digitus

interruptus from rigid Muff), Leschi
ignoring cop continues his demonic
attack on Yesler and waterfront. The cop
unable to solicit help, as
all hold freeze, launches into "Indian
Love Call" which awakens Muff (much
to Mac's relief), who is
in real life a beautiful octoroon Nisqually
princess studying voice at Cornish
School and she (loving men in
uniform) responds with Kundry's seduction
aria from "Parsifal" which
baffles cop until they get together in
duet of "God Bless America (and nobody
else)." They exit (after encores) to
an emergency cop phone and call
the riot squad which
comes and pounds Leschi (who continues throughout
chanting and prancing oddly about banging,
poking with tomahawk and harpoon until
subdued) to Burgerchef tenderized consistency, as
camera pans from business-as-usual at
Yesler and waterfront while the traffic cop is
locked with Muff in an inarresting sex
arrangement, as (close up)
jellyfish undulate in bay.

Scene two opens in courtroom, as
prosecutor concludes, ". . . from every
lamppost, by the good Lord above we'll
have law and order in this
land." The jury goes
berserk, foreman grabs up a flag, others
produce fife and drum, all march and sing "Yankee
Doodle" around the courtroom. Spectators remain
calm though fuddled. As Public Defender
shrieks, "My client, even though a filthy, backward
savage, pleads not guilty, but
personally I wasn't at the scene of
the crime so
it's hard for me to say."
Jury starts up again but judge

35

gestures hypnotically with
outstretched palm. "What," he asks
Leschi, "have *you* to say?"
Leschi gestures hypnotically (gives
judge the finger) and shouts *White Mother*
fucker; sees a black cop, *Black Mother*
fucker; Cop keeps stoneyphizz but
straightens smart black leather
cravat and adjusts smart black leather
ammo holster belt, resting
hand on revolver butt, eyes
smiling *Man it more blessed*
to give (shit) than receive (it)—
every motherfucker for himself
(sings "Ol' Man River").
Public Defender interjects to
(bug eyed, outraged) judge
"My client means this
whole thing is mistaken, he's
just an actor studying his
role on the street, but
personally I wasn't at the scene of
the crime so
it's hard for me to say."
Pandemonium again, until
Prosecutor cries, "Objection, his
act's too good, Yesler Street's no
stage for pissant players to
buggar traffic while
they hone their mocking
methods . . . We're witness here
to muckrakery and (reason)
treason spreading *seeds* throughout the land. I
call on witnesses to (lie)
testify: this bad good actor's stopped
up traffic . . . *He whomped my hood, Dented*
my truck, Was up to no
good, Why he said fuck! Too
much! The judge leaps up shrieking, "If
niggers can by God learn not to
shit in corridors and keep
a tight zipper on their fly (Black

cop covertly checks his) then
you stinking savages can learn to
live like Christians (jury
cheers, spectators, still calm and
fuddled, applaud) and (by God) you're GUILTY
GUILTY GUILTY and we'll (by
God) make you all good (dead)
injuns or know the (by God) reason
why" (Jury foreman leads "locomotive"
for Law and Order) as
(from Telstar) camera pans whole
of continental U.S. and
orchestra overlays muted "America
the Beautiful" on electronic reverberations of
Everett Dirkson reciting (in
unction) *with liberty and justice for all . . . as*
Leschi goes to gallows

and ". . . on the 19th of
February the unhappy
savage,
ill and emaciated
from long confinement and
weary of a life which
for nearly three years had been
one
of strife
and misery, was
strangled
according to law."
strangled according to law
the law according to
which he strangled
was law
(according to law)
and he was strangled
according to perhaps not his
law
but according to some (which?)
law
he was strangled and
according(ly)

37

he
dangled
from and jerked about (dares
Justice jerk her lovers off
the) gallows (?) That
act's tough to follow, but
before "a large concourse of people (there) assembled"
he (weary) according(ly)
according to some
perhaps not his
law he
(an emaciated method
actor studying the lead
for his own life
story) was
strangled
according was
strangled according to law.

Though few chiefs survived it and
"His (Leschi's) death may be said to
have been the closing act of
the war on Puget Sound,"
"(Kissass, stet) Kussass, chief
of the Cowlitz, (lived)
114 years. He
was friendly, and a Catholic."

*Seattle is described as a dignified and venerable personage,
whose carriage reminded the western man of Senator Benton;
but I doubt if the Missouri senator would have recognized
himself . . . in this naked savage who conversed only in signs
and grunts.*

Sealth, your brazen
image labors now beneath the
bowels of pigeons, or
now and then a gull will
bring you tidbits from the
bay. Your moulded eyeballs gaze
on produce of the land you've
vanished from—at this post card skid
road square, at tourists, sailors, cops, sullen
indians, and reeking Yesler
bums. Chief, my (suburban) youth was fed on
myths of your (pacific)
wisdom. Our ancestors loved you (we were
told) and named their town for
you. You weren't (like Kitsap) pushy or
(like Leschi) mad. You knew
your place. And (footnotes to your history say) you
taxed the settlers (shrewdly) for these restless
nights you walk, your ghost
unearthed by (chatty) invocations of
your name. That fraud vindicates a
savage (naked) born and remnant to
the Age of Reason. You
learned the game. History footnotes (at least) a man
who bites a dog or an injun who
screws a white man without
contracting clap. Counsellor, even
though (poor bastard) you didn't have the
style of a (Missouri) senator, you
counselled well to keep your tribe from
war. The Dwamish fished
in peace, were dry and warm in
winter, and died a quiet

death. They
extinguished themselves with dignity. Knowing
your (civic) duty, you merchandised
your cosmos to these states. So
now I come to see your (memorial)
reward, to Yesler where your noble profile
sits, your
brazen headress gleaming
in the rain, and
your stern (prophetic) glare ignores
the shoulder (twitching) where
a balding eagle shits.
Nor mountain no
nor bronze nor
stone are monument
gargantuan howevermuch
enough

Though Crazy
Horse
emerge at last from South
Dakota hills, his
mountain blasted tombstone's
pork barrel boondoggle
DRAG
show, (*See Folks, step up, look close—*
beneath the Breechclout,
stone)

A concrete buffalo three
storeys high gazes
down a North
Dakota draw, hot
for cows that never
come
gargantuan howevermuch
enough.

Air ripper, jack
hammer, blast, beam, and
balls we shape
Mohammed in the mountain, lament and

scan the edge of earth: such
remembering—poem, plate, or
song—is molding
making all horizons take
cadavered shape.

Emerge at last though
Crazy Horse he
may from South Dakota hills his
ghost is
friendly.
(Him good injun)

Custer died for your sins
says redskin bumper wit.
But vestigial Sitting Bull, amused,
knows more precisely who wins,
how little the sea churns
or earth burns to pay for sins.
When Joseph, who survived White Bird Canyon,
Big Hole and Absaroka,
survived the treachery of Assiniboines and Crow,
was hounded thirteen hundred miles by Sherman's Army,
haunted by starvation, cold, spectres of extinction,
When Joseph sent to Sitting Bull for help
he, (the Custer killer) said
Joe, do you, like Crazy Horse, expect some miracle from these hills?
You might as well piss upstream
to keep water from the dam—
give up, man,
Custer was a bad scene from a (B) flick—
but the ultimate (comedian) is Uncle Sam.
No matter how the sea churns
or earth burns to pay for sins
the guy that lasts is the one who wins.

In 1886 old Seattle watched
the sun, at Alki, extinguish, ripple orange, warm and
conjure sachems, their shimmer, his eyes, visions,
shimmer trails behind the sun—Seattle, tired
and prophetic in his impotence, saw old ghosts (no
ghosts) ghosts in '66. He learned
from Jesuits, and mad Leschi's execution, to

41

read graffitti on statehouse (outhouse) walls.

Nor mountain no
nor bronze nor
stone are monument
gargantuan howevermuch
enough

*Seattle, this naked savage who conversed in signs and grunts, writes to
President Polk:*
*Day and night cannot live together. The red man has ever run before the
white man, as morning mist before the morning sun. But your proposition
seems fair. My people will accept the reservation. We will live apart in
peace. The words of the white chief are the words of nature speaking to
my people, speaking out of a dense darkness . . . .*
*It matters little where we pass the remnant of our days—they will not
be many. A few more moons, a few more winters . . . tribe follows tribe,
and nation nation like the waves of the sea—that is nature's order.
Regret is useless. Your decay may be distant, but it will surely come. Even
the white man whose God walked and talked with him as friend with
friend cannot deny his destiny. We may be brothers after all. We shall
see . . . .*

(this land is ours
or yours your ships your
cavalry confirm
the stars are sky is
dark our visions dark our
gods gone your
god grins your
cavalry your ships confirm
his grin it
matters little where
we pass our days your
guns diminish gods your grinning
cavalry confirms
it little matters I
shall not mourn I
shall forget my

god I
shall sign your deed this
land is my tribe is
blood this land is graves holy
ashes holy land is mine is
sacred ours
or yours
your cavalry your gods and dead
leave their land or graves wander
fields beyond the sun our
dead remain their dust is
rich with blood white
man the dead are bloody
dust white
man the dead are dust
dust prevails our
dust we bathe
bloody our visions white
man you will never be
alone be just
remember blood the
dust is not without its power.)

In the morning fog off Alki in the bay
Decatur's cannon prowls.
Dolphins arc before her dripping prow,
and from the sky
gulls crash clams against
the indifferent shore's rewarding stone.

Nor mountain no
nor bronze nor
all the elegies of man are
monument gargantuan howevermuch
enough

James McMichael

JAMES McMICHAEL was born in Pasadena in 1939 and studied at Stanford and the University of California at Santa Barbara. He teaches English and is Director of the Writing Center at the University of California at Irvine. Mr. McMichael has published poetry in *The Southern Review, Denver Quarterly, North American Review, West Coast Review,* and other magazines. He has published one book—*The Style of the Short Poem* (Wadsworth), which is used as a college text.

1/15

The rocks on my roof
Thud to the owl's dull shuffle.
He does not care
That I tell you why I do not sleep;
About a night
Long, there, beyond him,
Long
And sumptuous with stars
That measure,
In their going,
Neither mind nor cold.
Nor need you, if you care, be told
The anarchy of dream,
Of sleep itself,
Of the last owl.

1/19

I am reminded that I will die.
The memory
Is an atlas of possibility
Completing that palest vacancy —
The perfect Zero —
With sounds and atmospheres
Final but undefined.
My ease is to know that, now,
There is no room for me there;
And that alive,
I impossibilize, by my episodes,
The world of those dead
Who do not want.

5/20: INTIMATIONS OF HEART-SEIZURE

1.

From these constrictions of flesh
There is to be no reprieve.
And as they grip it,
I feel in the golden,
Thump-pumping muscle
The longevity of a cabbage.
It is to want to know what to do
When the rivers for the last time freeze.
It is to want to be
The Bear Who Could Do Anything.

2.

It was when they asked him
Was there anything he couldn't do
That the Bear brought his press conference
Smartly to a close and caught the bus.
On his subsequent history — if it be that —
We can of course only speculate.

If he had been seen
Circuiting the deserts and prairies
Agallop on the ten-league
Strides of his wild sorrel,
Homing, always, to the alpenglow
Of the Wasatch, the Wind River
And Absaroka Ranges;
Would it have mattered,
As one night he turned not altogether
Politely in his sleep, that his lids
Kicked open to his pulse, and his eyes
Flashed into the freeze?
For it may be, nevertheless,

That he did pass through the low air,
Ascending to his celestial
Template in the Northern Constellation,
Fixing his fur with a resonance of fire.

Imagine him there with your children.

from What To Do When the Rivers Freeze

8/26:

Wishing seasons through this haze,
I imagine a grand
Preponderance of water:
Scotch broom and fern bowing heavily
Toward the first fall run,
Whorled gutters
And their limber bark-flakes,
Steam rising from the road,
And from the chimneys,
Wisps of still another gray.
What are my sins in all this weather?
Accident is my substance.
Oblique remonstrances whip
Windward into rain,
Fear settles into sounds
As death, driest of rain forests,
Steals nothing of the velvet dampness.
And staying these metaphors of change —
Only the remembrances —
Remembrances
Of earlier severance from evil,
Of constancy, remorseless good,
And of the loneliness therewith.

9 / 22: A PASSION

Waking,
I remembered summer afternoons;
Our path
Tunneled in eucalyptus
And a softness of sun.
Soon there were sycamores,
Their leaves
Ferreting,
Cool,
Through the culverts,
The shallows of the last rain.
What there had been of you
In this sustenance
I had not asked.
Nor did I wonder this evening,
Wading through riffles,
Scattering fingerling from the head of pools,
Waiting, into the darkness,
For the last gestures of the trout.
It is only now —
Hours before the next light,
As I see the slow, circling
Shadow of an owl
On a thicket of aspen silvering the moon,
And think
Deeper, into the pines, across the creek,
Of wild foxglove,
Its stalks
Spiked with a purple
Still darker than His blood —
It is only now that you become
Some tameless emissary
Of grace.

from What To Do When the Rivers Freeze

10/12

Higher, in the lodgepole, red
Columbine is a month gone.

Even below the passes
The cold is now coming on.

But there it is easier,
The cold. Its artists of despair,

Its Donners, measure a brilliance
Glacial in its bald coming.

Here in this limp dusk, I think:
I'm neither ready, nor not.

10/17: BREUGHEL'S "SEVEN SINS"

You do not wait the Angelus, but mark
Each scytheman as he lips his dusty jug.
Full of the warming harvest, and of sin,
These leather-breeched transparencies of God
People your cold induction to remorse.
Lechery, Pride and Envy are, for you,
No fleshless metaphors of Fortune's wheel.
Your eye fixes pollution's quick decay
To crude-limbed entities far less than whole,
Vividly separate from their final cause.
Filial and afraid, you claim as real
These mad distortions of a time not mine,
Urging, in affirmation of our God,
The substance of a loss that is not death.

from What To Do When the Rivers Freeze

12/8: BOBBY

Awakened, you are slow
To miss the random drain
From tree and roof. Below,
You pull the curtain back,
Finger the lucid pane.
Beyond, forms in relief,
Whose names you do not know,
Merge, in the early black,
With blindness to the brief,
Still rush of distant snow.

from What To Do When the Rivers Freeze

12/25: IN A GRAVEYARD: BODIE, CALIFORNIA

Dead one, was it here you hunted?
Below me by half a hill,
A buck noses through the freezing powder,
Quite careless of history,
Of you or me.
Behind his foraging eyes
He knows the nothing that you now know:
A totality of seasons and temperatures
Undisturbed
By winter night fantasies
Of jade light, throbbing to the north.
He encounters only instance,
Sterile as the snowscape,
Safe
From the imagining of that last
Tumble out of time.

Which of us, hunter,
Should move away through these hills,
Looking to the slow, alluvial
Swell of the Sierra;
Which of us should climb the crest of the icy cirque,
Guess the inland meadow grasses,
And prophecy a thaw?

Quicker, even, than deceit,
These sixty winters severing us dissolve,
And I am cold.

Richard Lourie

RICHARD LOURIE was born in New York City in 1937 and attended Princeton and Columbia. He has spent most of his life in and around New York and works now for the New York Department of Public Welfare. His poetry has appeared in *Chicago Review* and *CAW*, and his first book, *Dream Telephone*, will be published very soon.

WHAT HERODOTUS TOLD ME ABOUT
THE PERSIAN EMPIRE

1

there are many tribes in Libya   some along the coast   some further
south in
the country of wild beasts   others in the desert near hills of salt from
which
springs of sweet water flow (all these are nomads — to the west are
tribes that stay
put on their land and live in houses).

2

Among the Nasamones each man has
several wives   all to be used in common   if you want to sleep with a
particular woman you put up a tall pole to signal your desire.
At a man's first wedding each guest in turn enjoys the young bride once
then each
brings her a fine gift from his own home.

Adyrmachidae tribal custom in
regard to insects: if you catch one on your body you give it bite for
bite before throwing it away   the women wear a bronze ring on
each leg
they keep their shining hair very long.

(the Atlantes are said to eat no
living creature   their tribe is named for
Mt. Atlas at whose foot they dwell   when
these people go to sleep they do not dream)

3

The Psylli   a desert tribe who no
longer exist   were near neighbors of the Nasamones: after the south
wind
dried up the water in their storage tanks they were left with nothing
at all.

the whole tribe voted to make war on the wind   men women and
                                                   children they
armed and marched out into the desert: after the south wind blew
                                                   burying
them all the Nasamones occupied their former domain.

                                                   further westward
along the coast is the great lagoon of Tritonis   from it a river
flows forming the boundary between the Ause and Machlae tribes
                                                   whose yearly
festivals celebrate Athene   all the girls of the tribe put on Greek
armor   split in two groups and fight it out with stones and sticks —
                                                   this to honor
the goddess — any girl who gets killed must not they say have been a
                                                   virgin.
these tribes do not have marriage or couples living together   instead
the women bear children: the children live in the tribe until they are
fully grown: the men hold a meeting then and assign parents according
to who among them the child most resembles.

                    (southward in the country of wild beasts
                    live the Garamantes who avoid
                    all contact with other men   possess
                    no weapons of war and thus have no
                    idea of how to defend themselves)

                    (Mt. Atlas   a slender cone rising
                    behind the great desert is so high
                    the top cannot be seen: summer and
                    winter it is never free of clouds
                    the Atlantes eat no creature's flesh
                    in the shadow of the mountain they
                    sleep their serene sleep without dreaming)

4

in the hottest place midway between
Mt. Atlas to the west and the land of the Garamantes in the east
near one of the salt hills in the great sand-belt are the people who call
themselves
Atarantes — the only tribe we know   says Herodotus   among
whom
nobody has given a name: only the tribe itself and the sun are given
names: when the sun starts off its day blasting their land wasting their
bodies they
curse the sun with dirty names — they have a thousand names for that
hot sun   one
for the tribe and none for each other.

(along the coast a headland runs out
into the sea   the Lotophagi
live here   the lotus grows here   its fruit
is sweet as dates   it is their only
food and drink   lotus fruit   lotus wine)

5

further west nomadic life ceases
the Maxyes   Zaueces   Gyzantes   live in houses and farm their
own land
the Maxyes stain their bodies red and claim to be descended from the
men
of Troy   westward from them the Zaueces live   among whom the
drivers of the
war chariots are women   near them is the country of the Gyzantes
well
supplied with honey   some made by bees   but even more by some
method the people have discovered: everyone here paints himself red and
eats monkeys
which abound in the hills.

6

These are all the Libyans   says Herodotus   whose
names I am acquainted with; most of them   at the time of which I
write cared
nothing for the king of Persia   anymore than they do today.

radio

8 o'clock: snow flurries
shipping guide   "cuts of lamb"
in Italy two trains
wrecked by a herd of buffalo

coffee: sleeping   head on
the desk   music
an erection from remembering
a girl on 116th Street

11 o'clock: letters to
Dr. Franzblau   "my fifteen year old
daughter refuses to kiss her father"
the old man very upset

coffee   a donut   head on
the desk   sleeping   the end
of music   telephone: "your money
has not been approved yet"

12.30   coffee   the Angolan
government in exile before
the committee on Portuguese possessions:
"is this reasonable?"   head on the desk

the Portuguese representative
speaking in English   the meeting
is adjourned   the meeting is adjourned
where is the news of the war?
there is no war   there is no
news   head on the desk

dreaming of Queens

for Sandy Darlington

I am in Hollis   getting on the black
bus   it gleams in the sun like dark fruit in
a bank of snow   black driver   his hands are
steady on the wheel   gives me change   takes my
fare   all up and down the aisle black people
chatting quietly and smiling   going
to the beach or home from shopping   across
from me a kid is reading an Archie
comic   getting a big laugh from it   I'm
looking for a job   thinking of my wife
"I got a gal she works in the black folks' yard"

sex in America

Sex in America is my subject
according to the movie   Clyde couldn't
make it with Bonnie until after she
wrote a poem about their adventures

before that all he was able to do
was shoot up cops.   in fact the one who at
last killed them both so completely was the
cop who when he had been their prisoner
all tied up   Bonnie kissed the shit out of him.

the meaning is: how would you like going
to the movies with your wife to see Faye
Dunaway naked   the meaning is do
you think his wife is the only thing Johnson
looks at naked   the State of the Union

the streets of Saigon are cluttered with Viet Cong
whores. Saigon is America Hanoi
is soon going to be America
every soldier's becoming a movie hero.

Johnson's already a movie hero.
all he has to do is walk in the streets
of America   all the women would
rip off his clothes and kiss the shit out of him.

cancion

Sunday afternoon along East 6th Street Puerto Ricans
lined up next to their cars like camel drivers
readying for a trek   are washing   fixing
up their bright maroon or black Fords   Oldsmobiles
in the afternoon sun.   Others are standing
around with cans of beer in their hands.

When word comes the island is cracking in half
everyone flees to elevated points   (the
Empire State Building   better yet the Cloisters)
except for the Puerto Ricans. Now they've begun
polishing all the cars. Their wives are watching.

Soon more Puerto Ricans arrive from uptown
children of all colors are dancing now and
laughing   the mothers talk on the stoops   then the
families pile into cars   eight   ten people
to a car   the children sucking coconut
ices   men with guitars and cuatros singing.

When the island cracks the uptown half sinks from
the weight of many citizens   the lower
half moves out smoothly into the harbor   smacks
a few freighters   they are all singing now and
the whole thing floats to Puerto Rico in the sun.

ON VISITATION DAY

to be shot by Negroes on Visitation Day
(after the table's already been set up
for them to sit down across from you and talk
over man to man   eye to eye how you can
help them out) right on 8th Avenue as you're
really hurrying to the meeting to get
discussions under way. Not because you are
Jewish or the color of your skin   but the
signal was given at noon   the sun at a
certain height over the sidewalk   "Now"   and the
sun was the moon   day was night   fires were needed
and just before this cancellation of all
conference   you were crossing the Avenue.
Tables pitched out of windows are hitting the
streets now like grenades   and you go up in flames.

bad day together

there's nothing to eat but brown rice
      or apples   or vanilla ice cream
there's no one to phone but distant cousins
      or someone else about a job
there's nothing to do but blow the trumpet
      or make a chart of my sex life
      or sleep at my desk
there's nothing to drink but coffee or tea without milk
there's nothing to think about but how to get better
      or moving to the country
      or why we can't talk together
there's nothing to say but   I have to wash my socks
      or   what's the matter
      or   I don't feel like it
here's nothing to decide but when do you want to go to sleep

Barbara Harr

BARBARA HARR was born in Nigeria in the "very late 1930's" but grew up in and around Chicago. She lives in New York where she works as an editor. Her poetry regularly appears in literary magazines, including *Choice*, *Chicago Review*, *Prairie Schooner*, and *Tri-Quarterly*. Miss Harr has held fellowships from Breadloaf, the New York City YM-YWHA, and Yaddo and has taught in writing workshops at the University of Montana, Wright City College, and Hunter College. Her first collection of poetry, now ready for publication, won the Castagnola Award of the Poetry Society of America.

RAPID TRANSIT

A mile away, the subways rise
into the light, and move among
the leaning stairs of tenements:
close to a quarrel in a house,
children at supper, worn-out loves
asleep behind a broken shade.

I called to you, one evening,
across a subway station.
You could not hear, and shrugged aside
my last words of the night.

Sweet, we were born to eat, to sleep,
perhaps to dream a while,

to ride where blind men tap
their tin cups down the aisles
with songs of love and death,

to run, packed into crowds
where loonies touch our thighs
or doors close on our fingers,

to punch a transfer home
up the stairs of signboards
unpatrolled, alone.

RETURNING LATE PAST THE SUBWAY SHOPS

I ride the vaulted tunnels home,
having left the man
whose word can leave my tongue
a petal torn of lies.

The florist's stall is closed.
A dim light warns the few
who would be thieves of flowers.
Cornflowers, here, for the poor,
roses for the solvent,
and all degrees of blossoming
(I have loved gardenias
just for their brownward turning
about the fingertips) —
orchids, purple at the throat,
padded wet in cotton.

Blocks from home, I count the stems
kept till another trading day
when young men may be richer
or honest girls may buy their own.

Locked, in the night, these flowers
are each man's own to take.
And they are mine to count:
my ice-box full of roses.

CLARK STREET

A crooked block from home, the gay boys go
past derelict buildings waiting for the wrecker

where the poignance of improvement blows about
like litter in March wind. The city's money
ends aberration, sets up family housing.

Under these steps no children play. The doors,
lockless, boarded blind eyes, stare. Stiff shades
chatter like cold teeth in broken windows.
Chalk-scrawled walls, between obscenities.
hold shredded faces of unelected men.

Before the fall, I should like to have gone inside
the flats and passageways where men have lived,
seen the turnings of their ways, and gained
the unexpected knowledge of the dead

before the swinging ball, from chain, from crane,
in its diminishing orbit, brings the end.

POWER

The pale girls break
like watermelons
on the front of your face.

Watch the pink flesh crumble,
seed lie spit on the ground,
green shells crack.

THE AMERICAN CHILDREN

Dead men, in Manila Bay,
rose to the city's nets.
Photographs were posted:
family or friends could claim
flesh for a grave and candles.

The children of diplomacy
passed on their way to school,
scribbled on the pictures
and thought of pigs or Grandma

and later, much later,
asleep on a swollen ceiling
or in a fat manhattan
saw their own wet flower-faces
drown.

JUANA GUITARIST

I was those fingertips
    turning harmonies
by a river   two days before war

a woman, a guitar
(river is chilly, muddy, cold,
walk that lonesome valley)

blonde-topped wood
inlaid trim   geometries
measured silver frets

gut and silver steel
stretched to tension in the pegs
action barely touching

what hills what hills are those, my love?
mine eyes have seen   frosty morning
coral of the Solomons

if there was not war on the radio
there was death all around us:
wars in our fingertips

tenting tonight   the small rains down
cruel war is raging   may I
go with you   no

I am gentle sounds beside water
away you rolling river
bound away   before war

she died of the fever   her ghost wheels
alive alive   o   cruel death
give these things back   the dancing bones

these chord-changes

THE DRESSES
for Kathleen Fraser

Those gifts in place of preacher's pay:
potatoes ours for the digging;
chickens we had to pluck and gut,
pinfeathers sticking our fingers;

and the styles of ancient women
altered to our young bodies.

Kathleen, we are permitted to keep
any mystery or brightness
that lasted through the blueing.
Those dresses have surprising tensile strength,
more threads than you think, to the inch.
We can steam-iron over wrinkles
or crush them harder and tie the knots
for our own coloring
in op or pop as we please.

Or knot them into firemen's ropes
swung out of open windows
when parsonages burn.
Swinging to our own kingdoms,

a blister or two on our hands, no more;
then freedom, our feet on the ground.
Free to dance, to sing those songs
we couldn't sing before.

We know by now
that air- and water-walkers use
illusion or technology.
Our highest flying
may be our swinging from those rags
knotted into ropes
and strung from stained-glass windows.
Swinging like Tarzan (no, we Jane)

from vine to thorny vine
far away from home
with jungle leaves in our hair.

JUANA: THE BURNT FOOT

cooking   inattentive
spaghetti-water for supper
steady   without a sieve

blazing soft   wrinkles
shooting rods through the body
oily   tight

hold   crush the ankle
leg between the burnt spots
ice bucket when brave enough
our   rested   back in

pink rose bumpy flesh
skin wrinkled   draperies
thin white dead   graceful curves
pulled   fallen together
dark rose patch pulled tight about
high hard blister   deep water
skin purse full of gold
slides under surfaces
a hand can move it about
arches   gristle
thin ankles rising
axle rods   camshafts
spine sprouting out of them
roots to the ground   balance

pressure or it's lost
cut the shoe   it falls off
stays   caught in gratings
knocked behind a news stand
down a subway stairs

how will she travel   how will she walk
or float on spikes through Gotham
in slippers   boots   open skins

hand-fed animals

beautiful upon mountains
anyone's feet

Charles Doria

CHARLES DORIA was born in Cleveland in 1938 and studied at Western Reserve, Harvard, and SUNY at Buffalo. He recently returned from his second Fulbright year in Europe to teach classics at the University of Texas. His poetry has appeared in *Io, Chelsea, Polemic,* and *The Niagara Frontier Review* and his verse translation of *The Trojan Women* will be included in a forthcoming anthology of Greek drama. During his stay in Buffalo he was co-editor of *Audit/Poetry.*

THE GAME OF EUROPE: INTRODUCTION

I judged quantity as small because it was small,
because it couldn't so much as thinkably been smaller,
not with the gift of making the most of what I tried,
adventures qualified for the most part as lessons,
the spring playing over the senses was the recognition,
frequent enough to surprise, of promises never kept,
(a revival of that most valued in the earlier visit)
made with one so much younger still, consecrated for them
in none more so than by this private pledge
to form an occasion with the higher culture,
an elaborate, innocent plan, come to nothing, the account
lost of that handful of seed buried in a number of cities
and a few women, buried for five years in a northern town
of declining population, whose movements up are measured
not by the distance down or the widening across,
but by yearly increments of spring withheld and unrenewing winter.

There was youth in that, there was youth in the surrender
to the balcony, it was there in the young man's business,
everything was there that was wanted, that could make the occasion,
in her much-rubbed, high-held hands, the Roman nights,
the very taste of innocence well-pleased to think of it,
of the wine, the coarse texture of the napkin, how it grated
on his lips and smelled of its laundering, the crunch
of the thickly crusted bread, basted with white milk,
all congruous with the confession of all that they had.

They walked, wandered, and lost all they had, not having had
for years so rich a consciousness of time; looking, he saw
old ivory, and scarce knew where to sit, for fear of having
to use, the life of its occupant seemed, that way, charged
the more with passion by its age and velvet graining, "did
this come in before the wars, shall we speak of other days?"

It was the hour of evening, yet the daylight long,
the city more than ever penetrating the scent of flowers
in the streets, a whiff of violets perpetually in the nose,

attached to suggestion, vibrations of air, human, active.
as they were not in other places, the more and more
as night deepened and became of the texture of things,
and milder, a far-off hum, a click, sharp, nearby,
on the asphalt, a voice calling replying, somewhere someone
full of his words, not as an actor receiving passion.

Did they know, however their previous passion,
as it seemed fairly to stare at them out of the windows
of shops in the watery sunlight, the girls in them
blonde and red-headed as they were not on Newbury Street
the least admissible of laws, fairly to make them wish
things they wouldn't know what to do with, even if they were theirs,
the way it took him made him want more than mere wants, had he
come back after those long years to something only like that evening
in the Commons, watching the iron fountain unwearingly cascade,
a finely lurid entertainment of what no one had found at the end
of the process, it was the shop windows at any rate made him
the most free, better yet had they yielded to the appeal
of more useful traits (those first walks in Perugia,
pierced with detachment, flaunted no affinity with the dealers
in stamped papers or embossed neckties, recurrently shameless
in the presence of tailors, tasting fully of that leisure,
marking it as to one knowing it would not make sense
to tell it to another, to surrender it all to one more world.

1. Must you be near me when I write?
   The boy on the trattoria's steps
   strikes caps on the stone and the odor
   of powder hangs like the smoke
   in this room. He doubts it, he
   is not finished, rubbing them
   he fills the air with shooting
   a second time: 'ce l'hai, Paolo?'
   'si, ancora ci sono.' 'ma, che si fa?'

2. The trees have long since shed their leaves
   and Tiber, so high it seems the bridges
   sail against his tide, is brown and choked
   with the highlands like a species
   of Eden, like the german cemetery tucked
   inside the Vatican where Sig. Mattheu rests

'that followed, inconsolable, the lovely
form of his spouse, a mind of poesy
undaunted amidst his many friends.'

They were red-haired or blonde, and long-legged,
they were quaint, queer, drear, droll, they made
the city resound with their voices which had never
been so marked as when figuring the chosen language,
they twanged it with a vengeance, they drew from it
wonderful airs, to see to what extent the element
had reached them, and she, giving them the sign
for the hour as she had the previous day, just
as those in another time, the named, the numbered,
caricatured, flourished, failed, disgraced, arrived,
leaving, about the masterful, about those who knew how to make tisane,
they turned off, in tacit union, down the great clear architectural street.
It was in the garden, a spacious, cherished park, brushed
by a note of that immeasurable town, the tall bird-haunted trees
all twittering with spring and the weather, and the high parietal walls
that spoke of survival, a strong, persistent, indifferent order,
the day was soft we had adjourned to air, the windows
burning with late suns, the grass so green, wet, the shade scattered,
and bells tolling behind mist (behind the Fine Arts Museum),
I had the sense of names in the air, of ghosts at the windows,
staring from the shuttered chandeliers, buzzing, gibbering, too thick,
too fast, all the windows of sense, letting them openly drink in
the suns of a climate not marked in the Commonweal's muse,
the medallion marked in her face, every line told as tone and response,
in the manner in which she stood, in welcome and at ease, the claret glass
draws attention to her neck, held in the chausseur's eyes and speaking it
to no one, as if it would make no sense at all to tell to another,
this form of sacrifice did for the occasion as well as any other.

3. where the lemon trees

   pale smoke upon the hill:
   the third act, the garden act;
   the postcard, the five-tone plate;
   the faded lyric in the day book:

crisscrossing the yellow oaks
where walks meet, converge
where the hydrangeas bloom
and rhododendrons, sun-flowers
come up and glow among men: you
who are like the poet, another man
I have known, death like a young man
in the late sun, go to these dedications
though late now, where could I leave
(and not lose sight of that place
a gleam in the night, the fingers
like the lines, nerveless, not spoken of)?
if I have hit at the method
of a Europe I met long ago
in a hidden dream, though perhaps
a game, against the rules
of the game, setting off
upon the first walk, where
the lions in broken stone,
broken profile, carriage,
black wheels upon the far
street, dark rain, wheeling
after our couple (follow!
follow them as if in a novel,
they are the story) hurry!
they are almost around
the corner, no boulangerie if
they are lost, who will
sing of us, o Europe, I
am your hope, young man,
young woman, there is no
bake shop around the corner:

after the manner of strange flora on a tropic isle,
I was greeted by the odor of coffee, bread, all sorts
of cooking; that certainly was part of the day, that
first upon the walk, women taking their children
to school, in black, the flowers up, a leather book
in one hand, and lifting up the other bells ring ring

it was only, become them as music's part
it mattered, the main point where somehow
all there, indeed, the dream didn't open,
only the window, and my love came in, memory,
thee, of all most, I invocate! count first last
anything, that if it does exhaust, you go
and you do it

And when he looked he saw old ivory, and scarce knew where to sit
for fear of touching it, the life of its occupant struck him that way
charged the more with passion and become of the empire of things, the
lust of the eyes, and pride of the tactile nerve, the innermost nook
of the shrine, caught him as brown in a pirate's cave, in brownness
the glints of gold and purple, objects displayed on velour, nothing clear
save that they were precious and brushed by knowledge, contempt of the
flower given way to its worship, the liberty of the greatest concern,
the circles lived there as nowhere else, question as soon as they spoke
with the answer, the laughter quickly cut short, 'well, they've got hold
of me, I was extraordinarily glad to see you, one might live for years
here without a blessing suspected, and not to know it for at least
awhile is to need, or miss, it forever. You are that becomes the need;
and not to invite you puts it off until there can be
no fulfilling, no emptying of desire.'

THE GAME OF EUROPE: THE VIENNA CHAPTERS I-IIII

The law is in my soul,
I grow hot, I grow cold;
The closer it is to blue,
The nearer I am to you.

I. Land Swims Into View

If he with all his troop put in

if the boats glide
under the ranking trees
and sails billow in the wind
catching the steerman's cry

it is still as in the dream
the deep yields up her own

and it is laden with treasure, dragons lie
curled in sleep about it

the blond crow a human tongue
pecking at them, edging his way into the scrapbook
when all his fleet comes into port

from the elements a hint: how many?
in the garden over the seas
are the apples golden?
or the men?

beasts beyond touch go into books
flames of the snake the rowers sing

a golden age undrenched of rain
that whole yields up the moral beneath accident
into the valley past the glade
under the tree between dragon's teeth

                    five, six
                          charms of the day
                                stop and pace
                                      right, and go north

            voices, melodies, and a sleep
                  time turns to gold

                  not of them, not of those who seek
                        under the sun,
                              no harm to you
                                    while in his light
                  lighting a path, casting no shadow
                        coming, each armed
                                    with a golden spade

II. Albumblatt: Kitzbuehl

Birds sing and it snows
then are busy.
many times in the soup
the fruit either dead
or devorant.

"she is a baby hotel."

I work the crostic
in the Gaming
Parkstoffe Schlossallee
postcards 2.20 AS or 15 cents American
or five colored, or 25 cents for three
Where is Cortina d'Ampezzo
The meadows are clear and laundered
I fought in Russland with the Alpiner
sixty miles an hour legs broken
still brave as ever on both slopes
mud on the bottoms despite
imagination they continue
Pfitzner pain killer
dead soup fly

Cortina Lawina
Casino, Kino
Kurhaus, ich bin Gast
50 years before Europe
reacquires its patina
40 schillings and again 120 schillings

Low fire under the corpse
swollen out of dead belly
the formless will approves

German slot blur
the toil upon occasion
bear grey improve
the failure to set
properly may cause

The low fire flames from the corpse
sits graveyards midnights
the fiddler stamping
crows blackening
the owners stiffening
and the reporters took it up
in 1907 it was Guido Reisch
and then Erich and his wife
Erika, and then it was Reisch's ex.
and then Seiler, and then the British
and now the Americans, remarkably sane
if you think about it, Rainier and Grace
do not, and business has never been the same since
Kitzbuehl is near Woergl,
no, it is not near Woergl

For 12 years a blonde
and then another blonde
and he turned her out
just below that lift
to pasture
'in that cottage'
more voluptuous and a little stupider

than the first
"and takes in guests" mountains
and their effects on race

in my book
I marked that slope
1951

III. Wienerisch (Apologies H. F. Kulterer)

Caesar Julius strikes from behind!
Oistrach pays Paganini a bow
Fuchs drinks from Hitler's sieve
       We take the transit!
       Lethe is in spring!
       Time divides
       Death whiles
The old man Pounds his tongue in the torrent
spittle tempers his words
that have share of rivers and lakes
I slept in the shadow of Golden Helm
       In Victory no loveliness!
       Delight in endless war
       will in the end the world
       not win out in the end
       world in the death the war
       The moon is a wrinkled dug
       drinks the sweet air of cafes
       in the lair of man proverb
       smokes like the ancient crime
       Bale sink rise heal
       From whence this blueness
       Apollo's not this action
       crows, lift me as if I
       the corona upon the lonely sun
       set beyond that poets say
       rounds our earthen space
       Lights burn!
       in the fountains until all hours

until time comes and turns them off
good things from any side
in any direction either backwards
      Or forwards
      the water to wind!
      the wind to cloud!
Notes scattered
Day lady cracks
and the crows
depart, crowd
Stephansplatz
returning rest
to the Graven
      Cartesius!
      Maguol
      Pyramidus!
      Iambicus!
Pest soils the mind
that is constant
tuned to stone
star wracks
      and goes down to Hotel
      moon-sweat and, a man hollow
      beards root and King buries
to size the star
to weight the fool
to do it open-mouthed
      if not the tune
      the action
      rather both!
      and be off
when both are gone
hare and hunter
across the Tall
raze it in love
and eat the earth
      if not Earth
      the Moon
      and rather both

Dust rose as if from flower
Moon set and burnt it off

IIII. Epilogue for Dieter

Gloucester that with cold unyielding
Fold makes the pink and rose resilient
Unto granite, is grown somewhat brittle
at the thought of other seas, of
calls from the garden torn with grass,
across the stars her poets watch,
an atlas of the undead figure that catches
in its glare two histories in one:
the babysitter running in the grass
no fire, no baby, but the book's name,
important, furnishes the clue,
plus this, as if it counted:
"it was a god that rose up over me,
all fiery and fine, upon Dogtown stone,
pines crackling like tongues of fire,
their light floating my breasts in air,
no clear path down to either
sea or sky I could make stay put."
I will not let you rest, enforced
parenthesis, between another's hands,
though who of them that stand on the beach,
cursing luck, decides if it was whose?
brats that die tonight between her screams,
her spasms of delight; whose breasts,
beside the mountain's, that nourished her,
my teen-age nurse who's out for hire?
This then is not the double case:
do I go hungry if the trees feed
and deer have browsed on them?
Stars return the history.

Vienna–Austin 1967-8

Michael Anania

MICHAEL ANANIA was born in Omaha in 1939 and attended the University of Nebraska, University of Omaha, and SUNY at Buffalo. He lives in a suburb of Chicago and teaches at the University of Illinois at Chicago Circle. His poetry and essays have appeared in *Manuscripts*, *Chicago Review*, *Audit*, *Tri-Quarterly*, and *Omnibus*. During his stay in Buffalo he was co-editor, with Charles Doria, of *Audit/Poetry*. Mr. Anania's first book of poetry, *The Color of Dust*, will be published in 1969 by The Swallow Press.

from Stops Along the Western Bank of the Missouri.

A JOURNEY
for Ted Mallory (who died, December 1963)

I. Grace Street

Just north of Clark Street
Grace Street, disheveled,
without the regiment of red brick,
the houses, gray of old wood
stripped of paint above
the tilted, broken walks,
cracked by the roots of elms
that hang over the walks,
break open retaining walls,
that spread green over the grey,
light green after the torn husks
sift into the broken walls
and down to the earth beneath
the canted, cracked sidewalks.
Grace Street due east
across thoroughfares,
level to the Boulevard,
past a gutted store
with a drawn coonskin
drying on the gray wall,
level to the brewery
then down to the yards,
to the open sewer that
swills into the river.

II. Crosstown Transit

How did we move across the city
along the baseline of August?
Swaying in a dusty streetcar —
by the recitation of streets

from Grace Street south,
by counting hills, hollows,
by marking the familiar buildings,
counting store-front signs.
How far now in the mad dream?
Cecil's barber shop, Mason Street,
Rees Street across the playground
west, up its short hill four blocks
past my grandfather's two small houses.
We know the old black man asleep,
bobbing like a fish in the slow river,
sprawled over the yellow wicker seat;
Crosstown knows Mr. King's face,
deep brown skin stretched
over black bones,
the deep sound of his jostled sleep,
our faces, white and black.

III. Dead August

Dead August. I remember
the hard, cracked earth,
the street-sides full of dust.
The slow river runs scum
streamers from sewers,
hangs about bridge pilings,
seems almost still;
an old black fisherman
wrinkles the shadows of a doorway,
dreams of bullheads, long horns.
Clark Street at the silent turning
of shadows in the dust of August,
a passing car rearranges the atmosphere
raising a cloud of fine curb dust,
a carp breaks water in a swirl of scum
then slips back into the ages of mud
as the dust sifts through sunlight
into heavy air.

IV. Afterthoughts

The open land,
Indians on horseback,
the round hills rising
from the still dark river,
the horses dragging sleds,
women walking over open land,
behind the horses, bronze stragglers.
At the flats where the river bends
a party of white men,
a dark woman standing apart
looking to round hills —

Afterthoughts.   First,

the city in dust,
rain hard on the dust,
snow and heavy, white smoke-clouds,
dead of summer, dead of winter.
We move through intersections
capable of history.
Birdwoman, bronze lady of the river,
figure head of keelboats,
steel lady of bridges,
we pass in the dead of August.

THE FALL

Sunday in the snow
moving like an old man
I corner, slip and fall
with my hands out
twist my head to meet
the world I fall into —
present, precise to the moment
concrete, stinging, exact.
  The snow trees
feathered out with wind
across the damaged road-
way, Route 20, through
township, east and west:
points of my life drawn
out along the thin, bending
highway — dead dog in Iowa,
the bridge at Clinton
arched like a scimitar
across the brown dream river;
Mississippi, Mohawk,
Niagara, Missouri,
did I dream you into
the world, as far off
as you now seem,
beaded out, lost to distance
by the fractured road.

II

The snow trees are luminous,
the frosted globes, archaic
by the neon signs, come on
like a flash. Mid fall,
the fountain fills with snow;
I beat my arms in the air
like a cartoon cat finding
that my ladder is gone,

or do I remember, falling,
the girl in green
nightclothes lost on the highway,
the girl with the red eyes,
brown hair, green nylon
forced between her legs
by the base December wind,
screaming, help, screaming
with her fingers, red-tipped,
in her blowing, brown hair,
or an unhinged door on the prairie,
or old newspapers across a lot
fluttering, tearing on a cyclone
fence. The lights go on and I
fall hands first in the snow.

III

My world goes out,
dream, distance, picture
ice on the river, I know,
gone to distance, broken
in the inevitable present.
I am incapable of the present
fall, while at koolade
cocktail parties no one
gasps, stops for a moment.
It must be reconstructed;
I can not find the beauty,
can not stop it at the
point of impact, can not
make the vision, what I see,
go on from beginning to end,
can not keep it going:
the clouds move, grey,
around the blurred moon,
the snow fills the streetlights,
the highway breaks to pieces
like Mr. Ripley's glass snake

101

because I touch it;
it will not rearrange itself.
In the lighted window worsted,
in the sky the red neon scrawl,
Pepsi Cola — Drink Light,
I drink light, bathe in light,
fall into my broken world.
It is the inevitable order
that destroys, the necessity
of falling, river to river
shore to shore,
instinctively outstretched
hands to the waiting ground.
Those are my hands breaking,
dream of my hand moving
with my eye, eye following
my hand from the word to the place.
Seeing breaks the storewindows;
the streetlights and neon are
falling together in the snow.

SONGS FROM AN INSTITUTION

1. Wreck of a pearl-diver, old bastard
    gone to bad wine, sterno and koolade
    came home in '45 with tattoos for
    mother and Rosemarie; the jungle-rot
    goes sour every summer or in the spring
    when the rain stands out in pools.

    His wife left him in a year,
    said she couldn't stand the smell
    or even the look, it looks like leprosy;
    the mud and the water, he says,
    got inside me with the blood or
    deep down where it used to be.

3. I was at Iwo,
    beneath the bronzed men,
    there where it cuts off to the base,
    held my ground against a thousand.
    They hogged all the glory,
    puked at the groans of heroes,
    my own cries. The whole world
    cheers and cries for me.
    I am a soldier   a movie
    imitation of my celluloid
    march through the
    forests and marshes of Leyte,
    bearded with a cigarette
    slouched against a tree
    forceful, unconcerned.
    She fell for me right off
    because I spoke Chinese,
    took her figured skirt off
    and did a deadly dance.

MEMORIAL DAY

It is easily forgotten, year to
year, exactly where the plot is,
though the place is entirely familiar—
a willow tree by a curving roadway
sweeping black asphalt with tender leaves;

damp grass strewn with flower boxes,
canvas chairs, darkskinned old ladies
circling in draped black crepe family stones,
fingers cramped red at the knuckles, discolored
nails, fresh soil for new plants, old rosaries;

such fingers kneading the damp earth gently down
on new roots, black humus caught in grey hair
brushed back, and the single water faucet,
·   birdlike upon its grey pipe stem,
a stream opening at its foot.

We know the stories that are told,
by starts and stops, by bent men at strange joy
regarding the precise enactments of their own
gesturings. And among the women there will be
a naming of families, a counting off, an ordering.

The morning may be brilliant; the season
is one of brilliances—sunlight through
the fountained willow behind us, its splayed
shadow spreading westward, our shadows westward,
irregular across damp grass, the close-set stones.

It may be that since our walk there is faltering,
moving in careful steps around snow-on-the-mountain,
bluebells and zebragrass toward that place
between the willow and the waterfaucet, the way
is lost, that we have no practiced step there,
and walking, our own sway and balance, fails us.

A SECOND-HAND ELEGY
for Douglas Dickey, Pfc. U.S.M.C.

"How can I be bitter?"
the fence-rows rolling with the land;
the last full measure of Ohio
measured by fence-rows compressing,
through parallel above receding hills,
the mixed hues of damp Spring greenery.

"I never knew him to be angry or afraid."
that is, assured of a providence
moving within the accidental turnings
of his life, he moved with certainty
among the farmyard's familiar disorders
and occasionally outward toward Dayton.

"He glanced for an instant at his friends—
for only an instant—and then he jumped."
riding through Dayton on Saturday night
making the rounds, block by block,
the car radio marking time—
Downtown   Downtown—
the evening blush of neon blooming
into damp city air, the blue
clarity of mercury-lamp arcades;
four of them slouched in a Chevrolet
exhaust the evening, waiting for something to happen.

Note: In April of 1968 Douglas Dickey was
awarded the Congressional Medal of Honor
posthumously for throwing himself on a hand
grenade during an engagement with the enemy
in Viet Nam.

AFTERWORD

I

Because this is the first volume in a new series of anthologies, it seems reasonable to dwell on our designs and ambitions in entering the field with yet another anthology. In putting together this collection and planning the annual series of New Poetry Anthologies we have been careful at every turn to avoid making the project documentary or representative. A full documentary gathering of contemporary poetry would be so large it couldn't be carried, and when it was finished it would be of questionable value, even to large libraries. Representative anthologies always create arbitrary exclusions and tend to favor the poetry of schools and salons, which are often designed to demand representation. Both kinds of collections tend to create borders which are not poetic and, for the most part, not literary, having increasingly to do with age, geography, personal hygiene, and sociability. Such demarcations have often served American poetry well and have, on occasions, drastically reoriented the readership—especially the university readership. Our problem was deciding whether or not much service would be done by once again adjusting the lines of an already iconic map and slightly reshading its topography.

The decision was to concentrate on poets rather than movements or age groups and to give a small group of poets each year a substantial and uncrowded introduction to American readers. We excluded only poets who had already published books of poetry. The emphasis, therefore, is not on the comparative youth of the poets included, but rather on the fact that they all stand in similar positions with regard to their own careers as poets. All have had some experience with little magazines and quarterlies, and all have book manuscripts completed or in advanced stages of preparation. Because of its format the anthology also excludes the single-poem poet. There is little need to apologize for this exclusion, however, since such poets have the magazines entirely at their disposal.

It has become a matter of anthological decorum for an editor
to apologize for the intrusions of his taste into the solemn
and purportedly objective business of anthologizing, but
there is no way to disguise the fact that an editor's job is
judgment. People who are not in the habit of judging poems
don't become editors. If this were not so, anthologies
would be monstrously large and practically useless. We have
kept the rules for the New Poetry Anthologies simple, so
that no one would be turned out by the mechanism alone.
In doing so we have made the way clear for the poet and
clear for ourselves. We have also hopefully left the way
clear for the reader by providing the best possible way to
judge a poet's work—space enough to accommodate the
mind to a new vision and time enough to adjust the ear to a
new voice without the oppressive horizon of a just-com-
pleted short story or the clatter of dozens of other poets.

II

Despite the proclamations of a few poets and critics that we
have long since entered the post-modern period of American
letters, there is little evidence that modernism is dead or even
dying. The tradition of Pound, Eliot, Williams, Stevens, and
their contemporaries is very much alive and working in
nearly all of the poetry being written in America today. The
only real exceptions are to be found among writers who
proceed by notions of poetic propriety and not by any
scrutiny of traditions and almost invariably are enslaved to
that sentimental romanticism that the modernist revolution
set out to vanquish. Most of the quarrelling that created the
poetic schools of the fifties and early sixties resulted as much
from variant readings of the modern tradition as from
genuine disagreements of vision and temperament. I do not
mean to suggest that these quarrels were artificial or un-
essential; certainly, there were and still are serious differ-
ences between the poets unofficially presided over by Robert
Lowell and the late Delmore Schwartz and the Black Moun-
tain Poets, the Beats, and the New York School. What I
want to notice here is that such diverse and mutually an-
tagonistic company could look to the same set of earlier

writers for justifications of their several positions. This curious state of affairs, resembling in many ways a family quarrel, demonstrated the richness and complexity of the tradition that had been breathing down everybody's neck. If Robert Lowell, Charles Olson, and Frank O'Hara all looked to William Carlos Williams as a master, from outside the field of battle Williams began to look like a complex source and not merely a master. What was true of Williams, whose real strengths became most apparent in this period, was also true of Pound, Stevens, Crane, and even Eliot. The modern tradition, which American pedagogy seemed intent on keeping perpetually youthful, had come of age. If a generation of American poets could quarrel over the actual intentions, the crucial thrusts, and the formal legacies of a few major poets, perhaps the time was right for an emerging generation of poets to notice that those same major figures could be used variously without the internecine warfare that always results from the two-way proprietorships of pupil and master.

This new freedom of access has its own burdens; the more coherent and dictatorial a poetic tradition, the more secure a poet can be in his own traditional competence. The long lived dominence of certain features of modernist versifica-tion have made competence common in the last few years. There are hundreds of poets in America who can make a respectable free verse or syllabic line and scores who can protract a complicated metaphor, catalogue surreal images with alliterative authority, or get a fix on a Freudian ana-logue to their own painful experiences. Everyone must find his own place in a tradition which has become diffuse; the acceptance of strategies of presentation and modes of com-position are forced into a new area of discretion, and each formula must be questioned separately. Competent modern-ism seems no longer an issue worthy of sustained interest because the architecture of that competence is no longer monolithic and universally blessed.

The poets of this anthology seem to me to have benefited from this diffusion without having lost their own ways in it. There is no poet here who appears enslaved or overwhelmed by any part of the tradition, nor do I find any so awash in possibilities that his performance is merely ecclectic. In every case the relationships sustained here to the first half of the century are complex and often marvellously casual and unself-conscious.

Charles Doria's "Vienna Chapters" clearly have roots in Pound's London poems and in the *Cantos*, but that debt takes no precedence over Doria's own substantive business, nor does it produce in the poem's utterance any of the arduous Poundsmanship of diction and imagery that has been so common in recent years. Similarly, Peter Michelson's *Pacific Plainsong* uses a multiple persona that is easily traced to Pound and Williams. In its use of H. H. Bancroft's text as an intermediary voice at the opening of the sequence, the poem is reminiscent of Pound's use of Divus' voice in the first Canto, but it is also very clear that Michelson's poem has an independent purpose which this indebtedness will not allay. The poem's localism and its use of history are precedented in the recent past, but their own urgencies very quickly make precedent of at least secondary concern. It is almost impossible to trace out mechanically the sources for Dennis Schmitz' poetry, even though he is plainly and resonantly in the tradition of the imagists. The prominence of the image is clear enough, but it has lost here its sentimental tyranny over the poem, bound as it is by syntax and form, instead of analogy, to objects which perception and memory crowd around it. Schmitz calls this practice "double exposure," suggesting not only the mind's habitual overlay of images, but also a technique for breaking down the autonomous opacity of the image as set down in the poem. The result is not merely a version of shared image composition, but combined images which are mutually generative—an exciting and original alternative to the dead end posed for historic imagism by the autonomous image.

Among the other poets presented, there are similar possibilities for seeing major modernist practices used with equal independence. Frequently the influences are so well digested that no easily recited examples are available. Knowing that James McMichael was a student of Yvor Winters at Stanford makes it tempting to see Winters' hand in the hard-edged treatment of diction and metaphor in "A Passion" or "Intimations of Heart-Seizure." Both poems are, however, so much McMichael's that such Winters hunting would be a purely retrospective exercise. William Moebius' learning, like Charles Doria's, is unmistakable in the surfaces of his odes and elegies, though it is not obtrusive or excessively allusive and never breaks the quick, colloquial movement of the poems. Moebius has taken a special limpidity from his classical sources that always presides. The collisions with the mundane and trivial that are sustained in the poetry of Barbara Harr and Richard Lourie lie within the special province of modern poetry. Their imprints are so different, though, that the common ground extends no further than the direction of attention to these kinds of occurrences. In "What Herodotus Told Me About the Persian Empire" Lourie takes the technique of flat, almost prose-like encounter into an area most frequently reserved for poetry's most reverential tones and in Barbara Harr's Juana poems the concentration on the domestic and the personal accomplish in a second person another kind of mythic intensity which is also spared the intrusions of the rhetorical myth-talking voice.

I have concentrated on only one characteristic in discussing these poets—their ability to measure out a place for themselves under the still steady reign of modernism without falling to slavish imitation or self-conscious school building. Certainly this is only one of the qualities worth noting among them, and perhaps I have done them a disservice by drawing my lines backward instead of forward. In poetry, though, the two directions are always somehow intimate. The poet always plays to at least two ghostly galleries, one past and one future, which flank his mostly oblivious present audience.

M. A.